LIGHTNING BOLT BOOKS™

Meet a Baby Pig

Jennifer Boothroyd

Lerner Publications • Minneapolis

For friends at Gale Woods Farm

Lerner Publications Company
A division of Lerner Publishing Group, Inc.
241 First Avenue North
Minneapolis, MN 55401 USA

For reading levels and more information, look up this title at www.lernerbooks.com.

Library of Congress Cataloging-in-Publication Data

The Cataloging-in-Publication Data for *Meet a Baby Pig* is on file at the Library of Congress.
ISBN 978-1-5124-0799-0 (lib. bdg.)
ISBN 978-1-5124-1239-0 (pbk.)
ISBN 978-1-5124-1028-0 (EB pdf)

Manufactured in the United States of America
1 – BP – 7/15/16

Table of Contents

Plenty of Piglets

Look at all those piglets. Sows give birth to litters of piglets. Usually six to twelve piglets are in a litter. That's a really big family!

Sows build nests before their babies are born. Sows use their noses to push straw around into a special spot. After almost four months, the piglets are born.

This sow made a comfortable nest for her piglets.

Piglets can walk right away when they are born. They use their excellent sense of smell to find the sow's teats. They drink milk from their mother.

Sows can feed many babies at once.

Farmers help when piglets
are born. Farmers clean
each piglet.

A farmer makes
sure the piglets are
dry and healthy.

Farmers make sure the piglets have a warm spot in their pen. This lamp gives off lots of heat.

A farmer also marks the piglets' ears. The marks show the order in which the piglets were born.

Ear marks help tell pigs apart.

Some pigs have ears that stand up. Other pigs have ears that flop down. This depends on the pig's breed.

There are many different breeds of pigs. A pig's size and coloring also depend on its breed.

These piglets are called Tamworth and Berkshire pigs.

Getting Bigger

Piglets grow quickly. A piglet weighs about 3 pounds (1.4 kilograms) when it is born. It gains about 3 pounds each week until it is one month old.

These piglets are one month old.

These piglets have started eating corn.

The older piglets still drink milk from their mother. Farmers give them small bits of solid food too.

As they grow bigger, piglets explore their pens. They root around in the straw by pushing it with their strong noses.

A pig's nose is called a snout.

Piglets play with their brothers and sisters. Pigpens can get noisy with all the oinks, grunts, snorts, and squeals!

Pigs are smart animals. They can be trained just like dogs.

Pigs learn to follow anyone carrying a food bucket.

Rooting for Food

By ten weeks, the piglets are weaned off their mother's milk. The sow is moved to another pen. Soon she will prepare to have another litter.

Weaned piglets are called shoats.

Farmers give young pigs larger chunks of dry food made from grains. This food has vitamins and minerals to keep the pigs healthy.

These pigs are eating grain from a feeding trough.

Pigs are omnivores. This means they eat meat and plants. Pigs on a family farm might get extra food from the garden. They might get leftovers from the dinner table too.

Some farmers feed their pigs tomatoes, apples, and carrots.

Pigs will also root to find food. They use their snouts to dig in the ground. They will eat plant roots, seeds, worms, and bugs.

Pigs can sleep up to eleven hours each day.

Pigs spend most of the day rooting around or sleeping.

A Big Pig

Pigs are very clean animals. They keep their sleeping and eating areas from getting dirty.

Sometimes pigs need to get dirty. Pigs can get hot very easily. A pig can die if it gets too hot. Pigs roll in puddles to stay cool.

Mud also protects pigs from bugs and the sun.

When a pig is about six months old, it weighs about 220 pounds (100 kg). Full-grown pigs can weigh more than 500 pounds (227 kg).

This pig weighs as much as a refrigerator!

Farmers will send most of these pigs to market. They will be sold as meat. On a family farm, some of the meat is kept for the family to eat.

Pig meat is called pork.

25

Some pigs stay at the farm. They will have more piglets. A female pig is ready to have her first litter when she is about one year old.

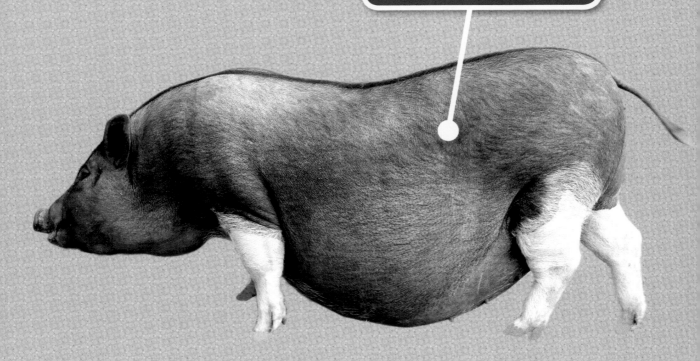

Soon this pig will have a litter of tiny piglets.

Raising pigs keeps the
farm a busy place!

Why People Raise Pigs

Most animals on a farm are not kept as pets. They are raised to sell or to work on the farm. Pigs are mostly raised for their meat. Ham, pork chops, and bacon are all made from pig meat. Pigskin is used to make shoes, gloves, and chew toys for dogs. Pigs are used to keep people healthy. Medicines and other medical procedures are developed using parts of pigs.

Fun Facts

- Iowa produces more pork than any other US state. China produces more pork than any other country.

- Pigs have been raised for meat for thousands of years. Pig fat was used to make lamp oil and soap.

- In some parts of the world, pigs are trained to find truffles. Truffles are a fungus that grows underground. They are used to flavor foods such as pasta or salad. Pigs can smell truffles from aboveground.

- Pigs with light skin can get sunburned.

Glossary

breed: a specific kind of animal. For example, poodles and Labrador retrievers are breeds of dogs.

litter: multiple babies born at the same time

omnivore: an animal that eats plants and meat

pen: a small, closed-in area where animals live

piglet: a baby pig

snout: a fleshy nose that sticks out from an animal's face

sow: an adult female pig

teat: a sow's body part that gives milk

wean: to get an animal used to eating food other than milk

Further Reading

Bader, Bonnie. *Pig-Piggy-Pigs.* New York: Penguin Young Readers, 2015.

Barnyard Palace: Pigs
http://www.ncagr.gov/cyber/kidswrld/general/barnyard/pigs.htm

Murray, Julie. *Pigs.* Minneapolis: Abdo, 2015.

National Geographic Kids: Pigs
http://kids.nationalgeographic.com/animals/pig/#pig-fence.jpg

Stiefel, Chana. *Pigs on the Family Farm.* Berkeley Heights, NJ: Enslow, 2013.

Index

Photo Acknowledgments

The images in this book are used with the permission of: © photomaster/Shutterstock.com, p. 2; © iStockphoto.com/anactor, p. 4; © Alba Casals Mitjà/iStock/Thinkstock, p. 5; © iStockphoto.com/seaspray, p. 6; © iStockphoto.com/johnmarquess, p. 7; © iStockphoto.com/rachel dewis, p. 8; © Agencja Fotograficzna Caro/Alamy, p. 9; © Life on White/Bigstock.com, p. 10; © Erika J Mitchell/Shutterstock.com, p. 11; © iStockphoto.com/phant, p. 12; © iStockphoto.com/IgorIvanov, p. 13; © Lighttraveler/Shutterstock.com, p. 14; © iStockphoto.com/taxzi, p. 15; © iStockphoto.com/Owen Price, p. 16; © Eric Isselee/Shutterstock.com, p. 17; © iStockphoto.com/Stieglitz, p. 18; © iStockphoto.com/ClarkandCompany, p. 19; © iStockphoto.com/RuudMorijn, p. 20; © iStockphoto.com/BravissimoS, p. 21; © Rasica/iStock/Thinkstock, p. 22; © johnpeters5555/Bigstock.com, p. 23; © Ed Hasting-evans/Dreamstime.com, p. 24; © iStockphoto.com/Kaymr, p. 25; © NatalyaAksenova/iStock/Thinkstock, p. 26; © karnauhov/Bigstock.com, p. 27; © iStockphoto.com/pandemin, p. 28; © Budimir Jevtic/Shutterstock.com, p. 31.

Front cover: © iStockphoto.com/anopdesignstock.

Main body text set in Johann Light 30/36.